CROCODILES IN MY UNCLE'S YARD!

By Shinai Bright

Library For All Ltd.

Crocodiles in My Uncle's Yard!

First published 2022

Published by Library For All Ltd
Email: info@libraryforall.org
URL: libraryforall.org

Our Yarning logo design by Jason Lee, Bidjipidji Art

Original illustrations by Paulo Azevedo Pazciencia

Crocodiles in My Uncle's Yard!
Bright, Shinai
ISBN: 978-1-922795-91-5
SKU01349

CROCODILES IN MY UNCLE'S YARD!

We respect and honour Aboriginal and Torres Strait Islander Elders past, present and future. We acknowledge the stories, traditions and living cultures of Aboriginal and Torres Strait Islander peoples on this land and commit to building a brighter future together.

The big rains poured
down. They lasted one
whole week!

The river broke the banks, and my street became a creek!

When the water comes up high, it makes my uncle Joe's life hard.

Because every time the
big rains come, there are
crocodiles in his yard!

There's a crocodile
near the shed.

There's a crocodile
near the bore.

"Knock! Knock! Knock!"

15

Who could that be?
I hope it's not...

A crocodile knocking
on Uncle Joe's door!

This story is a true story about Uncle Joe's yard on the Finniss River, in the Northern Territory.

You can use these questions to talk about this book with your family, friends and teachers.

What did you learn from this book?

Describe this book in one word. Funny? Scary? Colourful? Interesting?

How did this book make you feel when you finished reading it?

What was your favourite part of this book?

download our reader app
getlibraryforall.org

About the author

Shinai Bright was born and raised in Darwin. She is a proud Mak Mak Marranuggu woman from Finniss River, Northen Territory. She loves sitting and yarning with her family. Her favourite book as a child was *Four in the Bed*.

Our Yarning

Want to discover more books from this collection? Our Yarning is a collection of books written by Aboriginal and Torres Strait Islander peoples across Australia.

We know that children learn better, and enjoy reading more, when they see themselves in the stories, characters and illustrations of the books they read.

To download the app, visit the Google Play Store on any Android device and search 'Our Yarning'.

libraryforall.org

www.ingramcontent.com/pod-product-compliance
Lightning Source LLC
Chambersburg PA
CBHW042343040426
42448CB00019B/3391